Look Where We Live!

A First Book of Community Building

Scot Ritchie

Kids Can Press

To my friend and inspirational community maker Alita Sauve — S.R.

Kids Can Press acknowledges the financial support of the Government of Ontario, through the Ontario Media Development Corporation's Ontario Book Initiative; the Ontario Arts Council; the Canada Council for the Arts; and the Government of Canada, through the CBF, for our publishing activity.

Published in Canada by Kids Can Press Ltd. 25 Dockside Drive Toronto, ON M5A 0B5

Published in the U.S. by Kids Can Press Ltd. 2250 Military Road Tonawanda, NY 14150

www.kidscanpress.com

Edited by Stacey Roderick
Designed by Julia Naimska

This book is smyth sewn casebound. Manufactured in Malaysia in 10/2014 by Tien Wah Press (Pte) Ltd.

CM 15 0 9 8 7 6 5 4 3 2 1

Library and Archives Canada Cataloguing in Publication

Ritchie, Scot, author, illustrator
    Look where we live! : a first book of community building / written and illustrated by Scot Ritchie.

ISBN 978-1-77138-102-4 (bound)

    1. Communities — Juvenile literature. 2. Community life — Juvenile literature. I. Title.

HM761.R58 2015   j307   C2014-905279-0

Kids Can Press is a **Corus**™ Entertainment company

Contents

Celebrate the Community

Our friends are ready for an adventure! They are going to have lots of fun *and* help their community. Today is the street fair to raise money for more books and computers for the local library.

Do you play in a park near your home or go to a school in your neighborhood? Maybe your friend lives in your building or on your block? These places are all part of your community. A community is a group of people living together in one area. You live in a community!

4

Shopping Locally

The gang's first stop is Nick's house. His family is raising money for the library by selling things they no longer want or need. People call this a yard sale, garage sale or lawn sale.

Nick has put out some toys he doesn't play with anymore. If he can sell all his dinosaurs, he can make $4.00.

Nick will donate the money he makes. Donating means you give something to help a good cause. You can donate money, things or your time.

Cool Treats

Pedro loves going to Alita's Ice Cream Shop! He knows he has to wait his turn because some people got here before he did. It's okay — ice cream is always worth the wait!

But it looks like somebody forgot that you have to line up. Can you see who jumped ahead?

Ollie knows that pets aren't allowed in restaurants, so he is happy to wait outside with his friends.

Make a Splash!

Next stop is Amir's gas station. This is where Yulee brings her bike when her tires need air. Today Amir is having a car wash party. He wants to thank the people who come to his garage. All the money he makes will go to the library.

People in the neighborhood like to use Amir's gas station because he does such a great job — and because he is part of their community.

Community Cleanup

Uh-oh — look at the litter on the ground! Martin wants to do his part by cleaning up. He gathers paper, cans and bottles for recycling. Soon everybody is pitching in.

Being part of a community means helping to keep it clean and looking nice.

Grab a Paintbrush!

This is Sally's school. Art is one of her favorite classes because she loves to paint. Look at all the people in the community who love to paint, too!

Friends and neighbors are working together to make a giant mural. Part of what makes a community is celebrating all the people who make it.

Working and playing together help make a community strong.

Young and Old

Painting is hard work — it's time for a break! Sally knows where people are selling lemonade as part of the fair.

Sally's grandfather lives in this retirement home. She loves to visit him here because everybody has great stories to tell. Do you have an older relative who lives near you?

People who live in a retirement home have lived a long time. They are an important part of the community.

A Quick Stop

Pedro has to make a quick stop at the library to return some books. And he has another reason. He drank too much lemonade! Public buildings usually have restrooms for people to use.

Libraries are an important part of the community. You can go there to read and borrow books, use the computer or do homework with your friends. And libraries often have bulletin boards with information about local events.

Watch Your Garden Grow

Martin wants to visit the community garden, where people share a large piece of land to grow flowers and vegetables. Lots of people in the neighborhood have a garden here. It's a great way to make friends!

Today some people are selling what they have grown. They are going to donate the money they earn to the library.

In a community garden you can grow your own food. What would you grow? Beans? Tomatoes? Pumpkins?

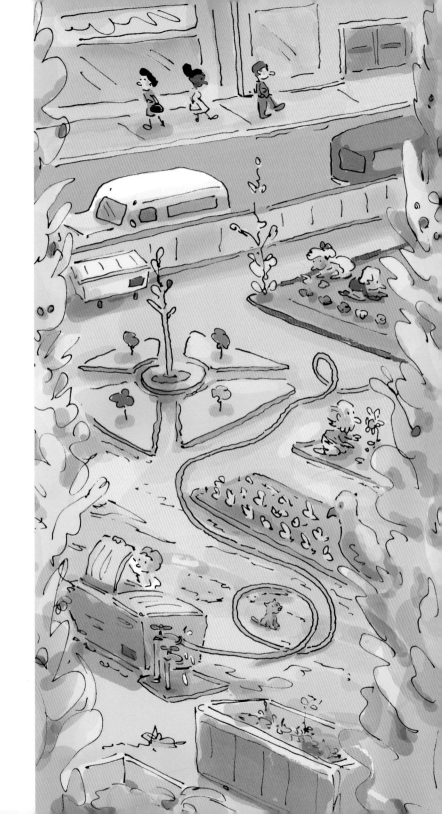

Goal!

Yulee likes gardening but she wants to keep moving. Some of her friends are playing a special soccer game today, and she wants to watch. But who's that four-legged player on the field?

Being on a team is a lot like living in a community. You have the most fun when you treat others fairly and work together.

Community Workers

Nick wants to make another stop — at the police station. Police officers help keep a community safe by making sure everyone obeys the law. They also help people who are lost, hurt or afraid. Today they're handing out safety whistles as part of the street fair.

There are many other kinds of community workers, such as crossing guards, sanitation workers, firefighters and paramedics. Can you think of other jobs people do to make your community safe and run smoothly?

Make Your Own Community!

When you find a group of people who like what you like, that's a kind of community, too! It doesn't matter if you're young or old, experienced or new to something, you can make your community better by joining in.

How about creating your own community? What do you like to do? Swim? Dance? Speak another language?

Everybody Join In!

What a great street fair! All the kids are helping out now, but where did they go? Can you find them?

There's no limit to the things you can do to help build your community. What are some ways you can help the people around you?

Make a Puzzle

There are so many parts to a community, but somehow they all fit together, kind of like the pieces of a jigsaw puzzle. Follow these steps to make a puzzle picture of your community.

You'll need: crayons, markers or color pencils; a blank piece of paper; a foam core or cardboard the same size as the paper; glue and scissors.

Step 1: On the paper, draw a colorful picture of your neighborhood or community.

Step 2: Draw a puzzle that looks something like this on the foam core or cardboard. Your pieces don't all have to be the same size, but they should be easy for you to cut out.

Step 3: Glue the picture of your community onto the blank side of the foam core or cardboard. Let the glue dry.

Step 4: Carefully cut along the lines of the puzzle pieces. (You might need to ask an adult to help with the cutting.)

Step 5: Mix up all your puzzle pieces and see if you can put them back together!

Words to Know

community: a group of people who share something in common, such as the neighborhood they live in, interests or hobbies

community garden: a garden shared by members of a community. Sometimes people have their own small area to take care of, and sometimes everyone works together to take care of the whole garden.

community worker: someone whose job helps the community run safely and smoothly. Crossing guards, sanitation workers, firefighters, paramedics and police officers are all examples of community workers.

donate: to give time, money or things to a charity or good cause

mural: a large painting on a wall or ceiling

public building: a building that is used by everyone, such as a library or a museum

recycle: a process that allows something to be reused. Many communities have recycling programs for materials such as paper, plastic and glass.

retirement home: a building where only older people live, usually in their own apartments